Pragmatic Monte Carlo Simulations

Chapter 1:
Introduction to Monte Carlo Simulations

To my family, for supporting me every step of the way

Monte Carlo methods, also known as Monte Carlo simulations or experiments, are a primitive yet highly useful computational algorithm. Named after the city of Monte Carlo, Monaco, which is known for its large and grand casinos, Monte Carlo methods use chance and probabilistic methods to make inferences.

The technical definition of a Monte Carlo method is an algorithmic approach which uses random sampling from a result range to obtain or approximate a numerical result. Essentially, Monte Carlo methods extrapolate many, many probabilistic trials to ultimately conclude a deterministic result.

Now, due to the rudimentary nature of Monte Carlo simulations, they have seen many uses throughout the course of history. The earliest mathematical foundations (detailed in the next chapter) for Monte Carlo simulations were put forth in the 17th century by mathematicians like Blaise Pascal and Pierre-Simon Laplace, who explored many of the statistical concepts required to rigorously define them.

It wasn't until the mid-20th century that the explicit formulation of Monte Carlo simulations began, particularly by the United States during World War II. The first ever conception of the Monte Carlo simulation was by Stanislaw Ulam, a Polish-American mathematician. It is said that while recovering from an illness, Ulam was playing the card game solitaire and began pondering the probability of winning. He proposed using random sampling to converge on the solution, which is the underlying framework behind Monte Carlo simulations.

John von Neumann, who you may know from von Neumann computer architecture, utilized random sampling techniques to solve mathematics and physics problems at the Los Alamos National Laboratory, which was used for the development of atomic weapons. Monte Carlo simulations were initially used under the Manhattan Project, where they were used to simulate the behavior of neutrons in a nuclear chain reaction. At the time, computing was also seeing a boom in innovation as well, and some of the earliest computers, such as the ENIAC, were the first to run Monte Carlo simulations digitally.

After World War II, the breadth of usage of Monte Carlo simulations widened, expanding to statistical physics, economics, engineering, among other fields. It became a fundamental technique in an overarching field known as computational science. During this period, other more powerful techniques stemmed off of Monte Carlo simulations, including **Markov Chain Monte Carlo (MCMC) algorithms**, as well as the Metropolis algorithm, invented by Nicholas Metropolis, who coined the original name of Monte Carlo simulations. These advanced algorithms will be covered in greater depth in later chapters.

In the 1970s and 1980s, researchers began developing **quasi-Monte Carlo methods**, which use low discrepancy sequences instead of random sampling; this less-noisy data sample reduces the variance of Monte Carlo simulations, making it quicker to converge and making is strongly suited for numerical integration and financial modeling which require greater precision. Most recently, Monte Carlo methods have seen integration into contemporary topics like machine learning, particularly reinforcement learning. Simulations can be used either to reinforce or enhance machine learning predictions.

Now, despite all of the aforementioned use cases, Monte Carlo simulations do have quite a lot of drawbacks which prevent them from being as universal as they could potentially be.

Monte Carlo simulations suffer from something called the **"curse of dimensionality,"** which states that as the dimensionality (number of factors and overall complexity) increases, the number of samples needed to converge on a deterministic result grows exponentially. Therefore, only rudimentary calculations and evaluations are typically possible with Monte Carlo simulations, as the computational intensity at the highest dimensions leads to a sunken cost.

They also typically depend on the quality of the randomization process from which they are extracting entropy from. Monte Carlo should ideally be done with a completely randomized data source, making the predictions that it is able to generate completely realistic and accurate. However, if an ostensibly random data source is used which isn't actually random, it can lead to skewed results that can provide subpar results. These pseudo-random sources aren't few and far between; they're actually very common. If you happen to use one of these as part of the Monte Carlo training process, you may find that method becomes much weaker and less accurate.

Finally, a problem inherent to random sampling is event of rare events in the first place. If there is an exceedingly rare event slated to happen eventually, it may take an excessive number of samples to be able to get a conclusive amount of samples of that event, which again refers back to the curse of dimensionality and the slow convergence of Monte Carlo simulations.

Let's take a common albeit impractical example: approximating π. Now, using an analytical method for approximating its value is very impractical and very computationally expensive. As an alternative, we can cleverly use a Monte Carlo simulation to bypass the difficulty of approximating an irrational number.

Let's imagine a circle that is perfectly inscribed in a square. The square has side lengths of 1, which means that the diameter of the circle is also 1.

Now, let's take the proportional area of these two shapes and represent it as an expression:

$$\frac{A_{circle}}{A_{square}} = \frac{\pi(0.5^2)}{1} = \frac{\pi}{4}$$

Okay, so we know that the proportion of the area of the inscribed circle to the area of the square is $\frac{\pi}{4}$, but how can we use that to estimate π?

Well, a possible Monte Carlo strategy would be to randomly place points throughout the entire figure and count how many land in the circle and how many don't. The more dots that we place, the more that the amount of dots in the circle versus the amount of dots outside the circle will converge to $\frac{\pi}{4}$.

So, all we have to do is simulate many trials of randomly placing an infinitely small dot inside of this figure, then eventually count how many land in the circle, which should be close to $\frac{\pi}{4}$. From there, all we need to do is multiply that proportion by four, and we have the approximate value of π!

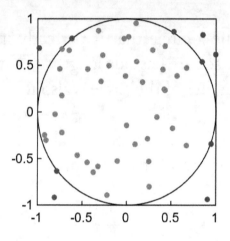

Figure 1: Monte Carlo Circle Approximation

There are a couple of main takeaways when constructing effective Monte Carlo simulations:

- Understand the problem at hand and formulate a mathematical model where Monte Carlo simulations are directly applicable in the training process. For example, if we are using Monte Carlo for numerical integration (as we will in a later chapter), write the integral itself and see where the sampling can be implemented.

- Use a random number generator source and ensure that it is a well-tested algorithm that can produce strong, random results.

- Identify a sampling strategy that either samples directly or indirectly and use that to execute the simulations and converge the model.

Okay, that should be enough context for you to get the high-level gist of Monte Carlo simulations. It's essentially a paradigm which allows you to use random sampling from either a mathematical system or a complex environment and use that to make complex decisions which are data-driven. We'll look into the many use cases of Monte Carlo simulations eventually, but I want to now discuss some of the mathematical foundations behind Monte Carlo which may better help you contextualize it. We'll look into the basics of probability and statistics, as well as a bit of calculus before diving into the explicit uses of Monte Carlo!

Chapter 2:
Mathematical Foundations

There are a couple of different mathematical concepts that you will need to know to be able to understand or at least refine your comprehension of Monte Carlo simulations as will be detailed in future chapters. Most of what we will introduce is introductory material from both statistics and calculus.

A random variable is simply a variable that depends on random processes. Typically, it assigns a quantitative value to one of its various outcomes. Random variables are typically represented with an italicized capital letter, like X. A coin toss, for example, has two possible values, heads and tails, each with an equally likely outcome. This kind of two-outcome, equally likely scenario can also be called a Bernoulli trial. We'll now represent each random process we come across with random variable notation.

Arguably the most important underlying concept in all of statistics: the **Law of Large Numbers**. The Law of Large Numbers can formally be defined as: for a large number of independent and identically distributed samples, its sample mean will converge to the true, population mean.

Let's take rolling a dice as an example of the effect of the Law of Large Numbers. If we simply roll the dice once or twice, then naturally it won't seem to converge to any particular value. However, for a large number of independent trials, we can expect that the sample mean will converge to the **expected value**, or $E(x)$. $E(x)$ can be formally written as $\sum_{x=1}^{n} x_i p_i$.

Therefore, assuming that the rolling of a dice is modeled by random variable Y, the expected value $E(Y)$ can be calculated as follows:

$$\sum_{x=1}^{n} x_i p_i = \frac{1+2+3+4+5+6}{6} = 3.5$$

Therefore, we can expect that for a large number of fair dice rolls, the average of all their totaled values can converge to 3.5.

The range of possibilities on a probability function (such as a random variable) can be described with a **probability density (distribution) function**. We'll describe a couple of different PDF's here, as you may find them useful for your understanding of Monte Carlo simulations.

The **normal distribution** (also known as the Gaussian distribution) is the most generalized bell-curve density function, which is often used to estimate the density of random variables if their exact parameters are not known and certain conditions are met.

The normal distribution can be written as a function of the distribution's mean μ and standard deviation σ. The normal function, or f, can be written as:

$$f(x) = \frac{1}{\sigma\sqrt{2\pi}}e^{-\frac{1}{2}(\frac{x-\mu}{\sigma})^2}$$

I understand that this is a very intimidating function to even look at. I think that the real magic of this function, however, is what comes up when you graph it:

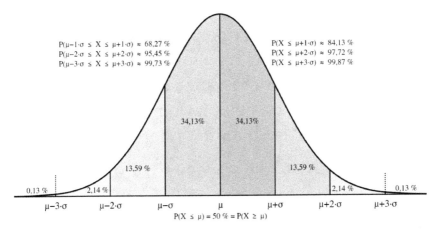

Figure 2: The Normal (Gaussian) distribution
Image by Wolfgang Kowarschick, licensed under CC BY-SA 4.0, via Wikimedia Commons

The normal distribution works off of two parameters: the mean (μ) and the standard deviation (σ) of the dataset. Using these two values, we can empirically approximate data as a function of these parameters. The empirical rule states that for data that is Normally distributed, around 68 percent of the data is within one standard deviation above/below the mean, 95 percent two standard deviations above/below, and

99.7 percent three standard deviations above/below.

Using a specific data value, we can also calculate how far (measured in standard deviations) a particular value is from the mean. For example, let's say we have a normal distribution with a mean of 100 and a standard deviation of 6. Note that we can also write this as $N(100, 6)$.

Let's say we have a data point with a value of 77. To see how far this value is from the mean in terms of the standard deviation, we can use the following formula to find the **z-score**. The z-score is just a fancy way of saying how far a data point it from the mean in terms of the standard deviation for a normally distributed dataset.

The equation for the z-score can be expressed as follows:

$$z = \frac{x - \mu}{\sigma}$$

Therefore, we can calculate the z-score to be:

$$z = \frac{77 - 100}{6} \approx -3.83$$

Thus, for the normally distributed dataset $N(100, 6)$, the value of 77 is -3.83 standard deviations away from the mean. Now, you may be wondering, why is this relevant? What is the purpose of knowing how far a certain data point is from the mean in terms of the standard deviation? The answer: it can help guide our understanding of how rare a data value is. Refer back to Figure 2 which visualizes the normal distribution. Notice that above and below one standard deviation from the mean, approximately 34 percent of data is captured on either side, or 68 percent total. Since one half of the distribution is 50 percent, we can naturally assume that all data points with a z-score above 1 (1 standard deviation away the mean), they are in the 68th percentile; this data point is higher than 68 percent of data.

Using this idea, we can use a normal distribution and z-score lookup table to see the exact percentile of a data value based on it's z-score. Tables like these are very handy for seeing where a particular data point stands within a distribution.

One final concept I want to introduce in this chapter is the idea of sampling, which is the process of selecting a subset of individuals from a population to estimate and extrapolate the properties of the entire population. When it is not feasible to examine every member of a population, sampling is used to approximate the characteristics and values of the population.

There are a couple of different types of sampling, each having strengths and weaknesses.

- **Simple Random Sampling** is the most obvious form of sampling, where every possible outcome has the same probability and there is no external clustering or bias to favor any particular outcome. In short, it is the most objective form of sampling.

- **Stratified sampling** involves dividing the sample space into groups of similar characteristics (strata), then drawing samples from each stratum. The strata are sampled in proportion to its size and importance, ensuring that all segments of the population are represented. Stratified sampling is often used for reducing variation in particularly heterogeneous populations where segments are not uniformly distributed. For example, stratified sampling could be used when trying to estimate the average income of a town; you can divide the city into three strata (high, middle, and low income), sampling from each accordingly, then calculate the weighted mean based on the size of each stratum.

- Finally, **cluster sampling** is where a larger population is divided into smaller clusters, then sample a couple of full clusters to be a part of the sample size. Cluster sampling is typically used when large populations are at play, for example over a large geographic distribution. An example would be if you were conducting a study on soda consumption in a large city, you could divide the city into different areas then select certain clusters to be a part of the sample.

Okay, that's a good amount of information on random sampling. One last theorem which I'd like to cover before wrapping this chapter up is known as the **Central Limit Theorem (CLT)**; it has significant implications for Monte Carlo Methods.

Essentially, the Central Limit Theorem provides an easier way to work out sampling distributions; sampling distributions is the distributions of all possible samples of a sample size n. The Central Limit Theorem states that if this sample size n is sufficiently large, these sampling distributions will approximately equal the normal distribution, and therefore z-scores and the z-table can be used to make percentile inferences.

In other words, given a sufficiently large sample size n from a population with a finite mean μ and variance σ^2, the distribution of the sample mean will be approximately normally distributed, regardless of the original population distribution.

The Central Limit Theorem is incredibly useful in dealing with problem related to Monte Carlo simulations; since sample means can be used to approximate population means, we can be more confident in constructing valid predictions regarding whole populations. Furthermore, it justifies using a small number of samples to estimate a population mean with reasonable accuracy.

Chapter 3:
Random and Pseudo-Random Number Generators

As mentioned earlier, Monte Carlo simulations fundamentally run on the idea of using random number entropy to make samples and simulations truly accurate and unbiased. In order to do this computationally, we need some way to generate intrinsically random numbers and entropy; programs that can do this are aptly named **random number generators (RNGs)**.

There are some inherent problems with true RNGs, that being that they cannot exist within solely the computer. Computer struggle to generate true randomness because they are **deterministic** machines. Computers follow strict, repeatable instructions, and therefore, if they are given the same instruction, they will produce the same result, not a differentially new one. Determinism is computers is incredibly useful for almost every other tasks; we want to ensure that tasks we give to a computer are consistent and repeatable in their results. However, this is fundamentally at odds with the idea of true random number generation; computers are almost entirely formulaic in their handling of tasks, and therefore, find it nearly impossible to generate random numbers truly by themselves.

Let's classify RNG programs a little bit further; for programs that truly do leverage external entropy to make random predictions, we can classify them as **true random number generators (TRNGs)**.

For programs which are deterministic but give the impression of random values, we can use the term **pseudo-random number generators (PRNGs)**.

Let's look at each of them in turn:

TRNGs rely on external, physical phenomena to produce randomness. These numbers can either be derived from unpredictable physical sources, or other natural phenomena. TRNGs are generally unpredictable since they rely on unpredictable natural sources, and are typically used when upper-echelon security and randomness is required. Therefore, TRNGs are often implemented for things like cryptographic key generation, where high-end security is mandated and natural sources of entropy need to be leveraged.

There are a wide variety of entropic sources which can be used to generate random numbers. Some of these phenomena are from physical sources: radioactive decay, thermal noise, and other quantum phenomena. The process of turning this analog physical phenomena into random binary data is different depending the data type, so I'll just take radioactive decay as an example and say that we can extrapolate this concept to all different types of physical occurrences.

To convert radioactive decay data into random binary data, we need to first start by using a sensor or machine to actually capture the data. In the case of radioactive decay, a device like a Geiger-Müller tube can detect the occurrence of the physical event at play. For radioactive decay, that would mean detecting the emission of a particular particle (alpha particle, beta particle, etc.). Since the timings of these emissions are fundamentally random, due to the laws of quantum mechanics, it is an ideal source for randomness.

Each event, like the emission of a particular particle, is recorded and encoded into a discrete occurrence. The computer can then take the random time between each emission (measured in nanoseconds, for example), and store that as a numerical value. These values put together, therefore, can be used to create a raw string of 0's and 1's, otherwise known as a binary string.

One important thing to note is that in the process of converting raw data to binary data, there may be inherent biases or correlations between bits of data, so it's often post-processed to improve quality. Techniques including whitening algorithms and hash functions are often applied to remove any bias; they balance the distribution of 0's and 1's and scramble the data respectively to make the data less redundant and more random.

Because processes like radioactive decay and others are generally very slow, they are typically not used to generate random data very quickly; they are often used in conjunction with PRNGs in order to provide unpredictable entropy as a supplement to an algorithmic PRNG. I'll provide you with a couple of examples of TRNG physical devices that you can research if interested:

- Intel's RdRand: Certain Intel processors have built-in hardware random number generators that are able to record data based on thermal noise and convert it into binary information. Similar to radioactive decay, thermal noise is another form of natural entropy.

- Some computers rely on random quantum phenomena to generate their predictions. For example, they may use photon behavior and emissivity to generate randomness and just like with radioactive decay and thermal noise, it uses similar steps to capture the data and post-process it to turn it into digital data. Due to the immense innovation in the field of quantum computing, this is a particularly promising option.

Overall, these steps allow for physically random sources to be translated into digital random numbers, bringing true unpredictability to computing applications.

Let's now transition to PRNGs, which use mathematical formulas and algorithms to generate sequences of numbers that appear random, but are actually deterministic and reproducible. Unlike with TRNGs, with PRNGs, if you provide the same input data, it will output the exact same deterministic result each time. Although this may make it seem less practical, PRNGs are much less computationally intensive and the gap between PRNGs and TRNGs is slowly shrinking over time. For lesser-stakes random generation, PRNGs are the way to go.

PRNGs come with a new set of terminology which we need to analyze. PRNGs are initially fed a **seed**, which is the initial value which produces the exact same output sequence each time if reused. Typically, to obtain the seed, data from within the computer itself (i.e. the time of day, user keystrokes or inputs, or TRNG outputs if used in conjunction) are used for seed generation. Nevertheless, for debugging and testing, seeds should stay the same to ensure validity.

Let's now discuss a couple of common PRNG algorithms, analyzing the strengths and limitations of each of them in the process.

We start out with the most common and easy form of

PRNG algorithms, that being **Linear Congruential Generators (LCGs)**. LCGs are recursive, and generate a sequence of random numbers based on a couple of different parameters which control the entire sequence. They are relatively fast and simple to compute.

$$X_{n+1} = (aX_n + c) \bmod m$$

In this case, the parameters a, c, and m can be chosen accordingly to generate a random sequence. However, there are a couple of problems with this setup. Random sequences of numbers have an inherent parameter known as the period, which dictates how frequently the random sequence will repeat. Since we are dealing with a linear way of generating numbers, this sequence has a very limited period, and therefore can exhibit correlations between randomly generated values if not configured properly. Nevertheless, for most general purpose, small-scale random number generation, LCG's work quite well.

Note that this LCGs can logically be followed up with higher-order generators, such as those involving exponents and logarithms, which can help increase the period of the generator. Some other interesting PRNGs include the Mersenne twister and XOR-shift generators, which you can research if you'd like further understanding into this topic. However, fundamentally, they all use some type of mathematical and algebraic combination of operations along with some inputted parameters to control the string of pseudo-random numbers.

An idea which we touched on previously but didn't fully get into was hybridizing TRNGs and PRNGs; combining the two allows one to take the positives of both machines and put them together in one system. Here are a couple of examples of systems that combine the two for better:

- **Hardware Random Number Generators (HRNGs)**: These HRNGs are able to measure unpredictable events from within the computer itself; the computer is the sensor. The random physical phenomena which they are able to sense includes electronic noise, radioactive decay, among other things. Intrinsic random physical data which is seen from within the computer itself is translated into binary digital data, negating the need for an external system or sensor which is able to sense other types of random data.

- Operating systems like Linux use a similar idea of taking data from within the computer itself; however, its data pools are not physical phenomena but are usually generated by the user themselves. They assemble and combine various pools of entropy, which includes various user inputs like the timings between keystrokes that they've inputted in the past, mouse movements, random system events and occurrences, etc. These pools of random data are sampled and combined in order to obtain pseudo-random numbers through binary encoding.

It's important to note that these "solutions" to the deterministic nature of computers does not rid that problem entirely; these generated numbers still aren't random and have some inherent correlations within them. However, by combining inherent entropy either from user input or from physical phenomena (inside/outside the computer), we are able to stray away from the purely algebraic form of generating random numbers.

Chapter 4:
Numerical Integration with Monte Carlo Simulations

A common application of the Monte Carlo approach is integration, a fundamental topic within calculus. If you're a bit rusty, integration is the process of converting the rate at which something is being done into the amount which is being produced; you may also know of the opposite, which is differentiation and involves turning amounts into rates of how quickly something is being done.

Monte Carlo methods can be used to approximate and numerically calculate the integral of functions that would otherwise be computationally expensive. This approach to approximating integrals rather than solving them analytically can be broadly labeled as **numerical integration**. Typically, numerical integration is applied to integrals where obtaining an analytical solution is either impossible or incredibly difficult.

A common example of numerical integration which you may be familiar with is known as the Riemann sum, which is a method of geometrically calculating the amount produced by a rate function by finding the area underneath the rate function. As seen in Figure 3, Riemann sums use a finite number of rectangles in order to approximate the area underneath a curve.

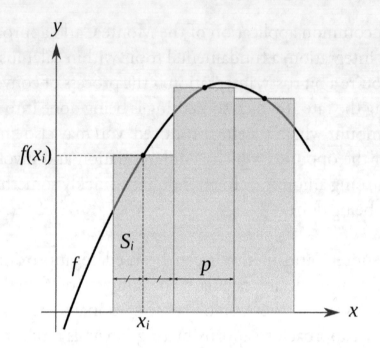

Figure 3: Riemann Sum
Image by Wolfgang Cdang, licensed under CC BY-SA 3.0, via Wikimedia Commons

Mathematically, this convergence of a function $f(x)$ can be represented as follows:

$$S = \sum_{i=1}^{n} f(x_i^*)\Delta x_i$$

This assumes that there are a total of n triangles between the two x-boundaries between which the integral is being evaluated, which we can all a and b. Now, if we place an infinite number of rectangles underneath this curve, we can logically correlate that the height of each rectangle will be equal to the height (value) of the function at that value, and the width of each rectangle will be infinitesimally small, which we represent with dx.

Using some new integral notation, we can represent this new sum as the following:

$$S = \int_a^b f(x)dx$$

As we saw just now, integral calculus is fundamentally extrapolating a geometric concept to the infinite or the infinitesimal such that we are able to make more accurate conclusions based off of that. Monte Carlo integration uses a similar approach of extrapolating the finite to the infinite, however, it uses "infinite" random sampling, or at least a large amount of it.

You may recall that the average value of the function $f(x)$ on the interval $[a, b]$ can be expressed in integral form as follows:

$$\frac{1}{b-a} \int_a^b f(x)\, dx$$

where a and b are the bounds of the integral. Just in case you were unaware, this is derived from the formula for the mean of a dataset, which is the sum of all possible values divided by the number of values. A similar thing is applied here, where the integral is placed in the numerator as the sum of all values and $b - a$ is placed in the denominator as the number of values.

The average of $f(x)$ as expressed probabilistically can also be written as $\langle f \rangle$. Therefore:

$$\langle f \rangle = \frac{1}{b-a} \int_a^b f(x)\,dx$$

since they both represent the same thing.

Now, let's assume that $f(x)$ is either an incredibly difficult function to integrate our outright impossible in the first place. We can approximate and converge upon the true integral as follows. We first multiply $b - a$ to one side of the equation:

$$(b-a)\langle f \rangle = \int_a^b f(x)\,dx$$

We can rewrite this by assuming that the random variable X uniformly and randomly draws from the interval $[a, b]$, or $U(a, b)$. For N samples:

$$\frac{b-a}{N} \sum_{i=1}^{N} f(x_i) \approx \int_a^b f(x)\,dx$$

If we generalize to the infinite:

$$\lim_{N \to \infty} \left(\frac{b-a}{N} \sum_{i=1}^{N} f(x_i) \right) = \int_a^b f(x)\,dx$$

So, theoretically, if we were to sample from $f(x)$ on the interval $[a, b]$, it would be exactly equal to the integral on that same interval. Now, what's the benefit of this? Why is random sampling better and easier than just evaluating the integral in the first place? Well, it's simple. Evaluating a function is much easier than calculating the integral of it. Think about it; you and your calculator can probably work out plugging in values to an ostensibly difficult function much quicker than evaluating the integral correctly in the first place. Now, you'd have to plug in a lot of random values in order to get a conclusive result, but it's still powerful.

Let's take a real example and we want to evaluate this integral:

$$\int_0^\pi \sin(x)\, dx$$

Of course, we know that the antiderivative of $\sin(x)$ is $-\cos(x)$, so we can evaluate the function using the First Fundamental Theorem of Calculus:

$$\int_0^\pi \sin(x)\, dx = -\cos(\pi) - (-\cos(0))$$
$$= 2$$

However, let's prove this using Monte Carlo integration. As mentioned earlier, we need to use a random uniform internal to randomly generate values to be used for integration. The integral setup can be represented as follows:

$$\langle \sin(x)_{[0,\pi]} \rangle = \frac{1}{\pi} \int_0^\pi \sin(x)\, dx$$

$$\pi \langle \sin(x)_{[0,\pi]} \rangle = \int_0^\pi \sin(x)\, dx$$

Let's simulate 10000 trials by sampling the function $\sin(x)$ on the random uniform interval of $[0, \pi]$.

$$\frac{\pi}{10000} \sum_{i=1}^{10000} \sin(x)_{[0,\pi]} \approx \int_0^\pi \sin(x)\, dx$$

As you may have expected, we can write code to simulate this process and see how close the approximation is to the actual numerical answer. After 10000 trials, we received a sampled average of 2.0095; pretty accurate! I want to introduce one addition on top of traditional Monte Carlo integration, that being the idea of uniform sampling. In the example just shown, we sampled uniformly from the interval $[0, \pi]$, which there is nothing inherently wrong with. However, it can be a bit time-consuming compared to the method of sampling which I am about to introduce.

Importance sampling is a step above traditional Monte Carlo sampling in the sense that it prioritizes areas of the sampling region where the integrand has a higher impact on the result; more dense areas of the function are prioritized. This not only makes the algorithm more computationally favorable, but also more accurate to some degree.

Let's start off simple: we want to integrate function $f(x)$ over an arbitrary domain D.

$$I = \int_D f(x)dx$$

In standard Monte Carlo simulations, we would sample uniformly from all possible values over D; however, if $f(x)$ varies greatly over our set domain, we may be sampling from regions where $f(x)$ has low density values, meaning that samples might be wasted in the sense that they contribute very little to the integral.

Importance sampling nullifies this concern by using another function on top of the integrand $f(x)$ which is known as the density function $g(x)$. Therefore:

- $g(x)$ is a density function over domain D, meaning that $g(x)$ is greater than 0, and that $\int_D g(x)dx = 1$
- The goal of our use of $g(x)$ is to lower the overall variance of the function $f(x)$ on the domain D.

Using this concept of importance sampling, we can rewrite the integral as:

$$I = \int_D f(x)dx = \int_D \frac{f(x)}{g(x)}g(x)dx$$

If we sample from $g(x)$ over the domain D, therefore, we should be sampling values from the regions of the function which are more dense, which means we are sampling from higher-value regions of the function itself.

Let's take an example of an abstract function which we want to differentiate using importance sampling:

$$I = \int_0^1 \frac{e^{-x}}{x + 0.1}$$

If you were to graph this function, you would see that there is a peak near $x = 0$, meaning if we sampled equally from the interval $[0, 1]$, there would be quite a lot of wasted samples. We could therefore choose a $g(x)$ exponential distribution function, such as $\lambda e^{\lambda x}$ (assuming λ is near 1), we would be able to plug this in for $g(x)$ and get an integral distribution function which samples values from regions closer to 1 more often.

In theory, this idea of importance sampling would yield a more accurate result with a fewer amount of total samples.

Okay, that concludes our discussion of numerical integration and some different Monte Carlo solutions to solving some difficult problems within differential calculus. We'll now look at how we can use Monte Carlo solutions can be used in conjunction with other mathematical methods to solve more complex problems.

Chapter 5:
Markov Chain Monte Carlo (MCMC) Methods

I now want to introduce to you a combination of Monte Carlo methods with an abstract statistical idea known as a Markov Chain.

Markov Chain Monte Carlo methods are popular techniques particularly in statistics and machine learning which are used to approximate complex **probability distributions** not possible with traditional methods. The idea behind these methods is to use a Markov Chain whose stationary (long-term) distribution matches the desired distribution we're trying to obtain and understand. By simulating this chain and sampling points, we can converge on the target distribution without an explicit formula.

A Markov Chain is a sequence of random steps between various different "states," and each step is only dependent on the current state. This process can also be referred to as "memorylessness." The Markov Chain memorylessness allows us to gradually explore the distribution by creating a sequence of state samples that can be referred to later.

Here's a step-by-step guide on how Markov Chains work:

- We initialize a random starting point (state) within an environment or a presented area with instanced states.

- We can propose a new state (i.e. take an action) based on the current state.

- Using an **acceptance criterion**, we can decide whether the new state should be accepted as part of the existing Markov Chain.

- Repeat the process.

Essentially, a Markov Chain Monte Carlo algorithm works by simulating a random walk in the space of possible outcomes, and uses a guided acceptance rule to ensure that over time, samples from the walk approximate the desired target distribution. The way that the acceptance criterion is chosen between different Markov Chain Monte Carlo methods is different, but it typically uses some type of ratio to determine a positive or negative shift in the probability distribution to maintain an overall high-probability distribution.

Just in case that description had too much jargon, let's simplify this idea even further:

Let's say we want to understand a difficult geographic distribution (i.e. a landscape or a hill), but it is too difficult and expensive to map out directly. We can construct a path (Markov Chain) which wanders around this landscape, and follows random steps where each step is only dependent on the previous step. We take random steps, but over time, we spend more areas in the landscape that are more likely to be landed on (high probability) than low-probability areas, due to the acceptance criterion. At the end, after a large amount of wandering, the points we visited that are compiled in the Markov chain should be a good representation of the original distribution.

Let's now get into some common Markov Chain Monte Carlo Methods, all of which have the same fundamental principles but work in slightly different ways:

- The **Metropolis-Hastings Algorithm**; this is one of the most basic Markov Chain Monte Carlo algorithms which still has many use cases for sampling from higher-dimensional probability distributions. The way that the Metropolis-Hastings algorithm works is that it generates a "proposal" with a new state relative to the old state; if the acceptance probability (which constitutes the acceptance criterion in this case) is greater than 1, the proposal is accepted and else, rejected. Fundamentally, the Metropolis-Hastings algorithm exemplifies an idea we touched on earlier with the ratio of comparing a distribution with a new state to the old distribution as the acceptance criterion which guides the Markov Chain.

- **Hamiltonian Monte Carlo** methods are interesting because they use improve on the efficiency of traditional Markov Chain Monte Carlo methods by adding an additional parameter to moves of the Markov Chain: momentum. Hamiltonian Monte Carlo methods are popular particularly for more intensive computational methods such as deep learning and Bayesian inference (using a prior distribution to estimate future distributions) because there is no singular, linear random-walk because of the addition of a vector momentum quantity. This extra parameter, in theory, should allow it to explore complex distributions faster and with more precision.

- Finally, **Gibbs sampling** is a Markov Chain Monte Carlo methods where you update each variable (a factor which affects the distribution) of a high-probability system independently so that we can collectively condition all the variables such that they work optimally. Typically, if we are presented with a conditional distribution with known variables that affect it, we can account for each variable independently and increase efficiency for higher-order Bayesian models.

Overall, Markov Chain Monte Carlo algorithms are powerful because they allow us to tackle problems in high-dimensional and complex probabilistic spaces; as opposed to exploring these environments directly, the indirect yet nuanced method of exploring them as seen with the various Markov Chain Monte Carlo Methods presented allows us to approximate solutions to problems with complex dependencies and other intricacies.

Chapter 6: Conclusion

And that concludes our discussion of Monte Carlo simulations! In this short book, I hope you were able to understand at least the fundamental principles behind Monte Carlo simulations and some of its practical applications in pure mathematics, applied statistics and probability, as well as computer science. This underlying knowledge should prove valuable to you and serve as a cornerstone for other, more complex technologies you may come across which use the same principles; sampling for approximation, scaling to higher-dimensional environments, etc.

Now that this book is concluded, I want to candidly introduce to you, the reader, some new topics and concepts stemming off of ideas like Monte Carlo simulations that I think you may find interesting. I won't provide all of the illustrative examples and formulas like I did earlier in the book; instead, I'll simply be introducing these topics and you can feel free to pick and choose whichever topics you find to be the most intriguing.

This book very lightly touched on some of the applications of Monte Carlo simulations within computer science, particularly within fields like machine learning, deep learning, and optimized neural networks. As I would recommend to almost anyone with a keen interest in mathematics and computation, learning how to code and understanding the mathematical principles behind machine learning is an incredibly valuable skill to have as AI becomes an increasingly prevalent and contentious topic within a variety of industries.

I'll start by introducing a couple of the most common machine learning paradigms, and providing a quick description of each of them. They are all relatively straightforward, but serve as guiding points for further research if you happen to be interested in any of them:

- **Supervised learning** is arguably the most powerful of the three primary machine learning paradigms; algorithms involve the use of labeled training data from which the machine learning model characterizes the various features of each label. From this training, a supervised learning model should theoretically be able to take an unlabeled image which it has not seen before, and assuming it fits into the labeled categories which it has seen before, should be able to correctly classify it, barring that the model has had enough training cycles and training data provided to it. Let's take an example of supervised learning: classifying images of cats and dogs. If we feed a supervised learning model 50000 images of cats and 50000 images of dogs and then present it with an unlabeled image of a cat or a dog, it should ideally be able to classify it correctly. The way it does so, on the pixel level, is it correlates different pixel shades, shapes, and lines together for both cats and dogs and looks for these same attributes in the image that it is presented with.

- One of the main problems with supervised learning is the issue of obtaining accurately labeled throughput data; for large and complex problems which require large and complex datasets, it can be difficult to obtain that much data. That's where the next machine learning paradigm comes in, which is called **unsupervised learning**. The premise behind unsupervised learning is that you feed it unlabeled data (it doesn't know what to classify it as), and by itself, the model should be able to at least cluster together data points with similar content. As opposed to classification, unsupervised learning is typically used for clustering. Now, this produces inherently weaker results due to the lack of a human-labeled aspect, however, unsupervised learning can prove beneficial in scenarios when there is no labeled data but you still want to analyze similar data points in some way.

- Finally, the last machine learning paradigm is arguably the most abstract; rather than analyzing the data which is already presented to you, **reinforcement learning** does something different and explores the data. Reinforcement learning can be boiled down to symbolic interactions between a virtual agent and its environment. The environment is instanced into various localized areas, known as states, and the agent can traverse between these states by taking various actions. The learning that comes with reinforcement learning comes in the form of sparsely distributed rewards (either positive, negative, or zero), which the agent can collect throughout its journey through an environment before stopping at a terminal state. The goal of a reinforcement learning algorithm, therefore, is to learn a strategy, or policy, which is able to maximize the total positive collected reward in the least amount of steps.

The concepts we saw in reinforcement learning might be familiar; when we discussed Markov Chain Monte Carlo algorithms, we made reference to environments and different states in that environment. This makes sense, as one underlying mathematical framework behind reinforcement learning is called the **Markov Decision Process**, which naturally aligns with Markov Chain Monte Carlo algorithms.

Note that there are some other types of machine learning paradigms, including those that combine the existing three, but these are the main ones. I strongly encourage you to look into any of them which you find interesting and understand the math behind it as well as how it can be implemented with code.

One concept which is becoming increasingly prevalent in the fields of artificial intelligence is the idea of generative AI, which is artificial intelligence that can produce its own unique content based on data it has received before. This can be by either meshing together pre-existing content or creating all new data entirely through a random process.

There are two streams of thought when it comes to generative AI: transformer architecture and generative adversarial networks, and I'll introduce each of them in turn, as both of them have immense potential.

- **Transformer architecture** is the fundamental technology behind **large language models (LLMs)**, which include ChatGPT Meta LLaMa 2, Google Bard, among others. Although a lot of major tech companies place their own spin on the idea of the LLM (with strengths and weaknesses to each), if you've used any of them, you should be aware of how powerful they are for text summarization, creation, etc. The transformer architecture was first published by Google in their groundbreaking paper "Attention is All You Need," where a sophisticated natural language processing system takes in text input and produces text as an output, by converting words into numerical representations (embeddings) and determining which words are necessary for the meaning of other words (self-attention). With many layers of self-attention, large language models can predict the next word in a sentence intelligently, and due to the vast datasets these models are trained on, they can pull from a wide pool of information to make incredibly complex judgments.

- If you're familiar with a mathematical system known as game theory, **generative adversarial networks** should feel right at home for you; they work on something known as a zero-sum game, where the gain of one player must lead to the equivalent loss of another player. A generative adversarial network consists of two different neural networks, the **generator** and the **discriminator**. The generator takes in a random input and conforms it to the output format (typically an image; 28 x 28 pixel for example), and the discriminator is given the generated image and the real image and is supposed to make a decision on which is the real one. As a result of this process, both neural networks learn to generate/discriminate better, and are honed to be as strong as possible with intensive training.

Just for clarity, here is an image of a generative adversarial network that may make the process easier to visualize:

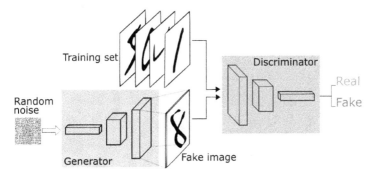

Figure 4: Generative Adversarial Network
Image by Thalles Santos Silva from A Short Introduction to Generative Adversarial Networks at https://sthalles.github.io/intro-to-gans/

Okay, that concludes our discussion of some new tech concepts which you may enjoy taking a look at in your spare time!

As the author, I'd like to wholeheartedly thank you for choosing to purchase and read this book; as a young, up-and-coming author who is passionate about the applications of combining mathematics and computer science, thank you for taking the to learn about and understand Monte Carlo simulations, a rudimentary yet substantial topic which exemplifies how a small concept can go a long way.

I plan to write more books on concepts which similarly combine mathematics with tangible computer science concepts (particularly AI), and I hope you will take the pleasure in reading them when they eventually come out.

Once again, thank you so much for reading!